Bureaucrats Who Block Progress:

How To Deal With Them

Comment on Cover Photo:

**When there is no viable path
it may become very difficult
to make your way through the jungle**

Jesuis Laplume

Bureaucrats Who Block Progress

2019 Edition
Copyright © 2019 by Jesuis Laplume

ISBN:9781532741050

2019-01-06

Also available as an eBook

Table of Contents

What Comes Next?
    Learning Who the Blockers Are
    Confirming That All Are Identified
    Removing The Offenders
    Rebuilding With Those Who Get Things Done
The Author
    What The Author Believes
References & Further Reading
The Author's Sites And Books
Your Notes

A General Caution

As one who has studied in many fields,
and learned about the limits in all of them,
please take the following caution to heart:

**It is both your right *and* your responsibility,
to accept from what anyone offers you,
only those that will make you a better you.**
***Those should be between you and your Maker
- no one else.***

Please take all that I write
as a reason to form new questions
about who you are,
as well as who you are meant to be.

***There will only ever be one you
and the universe won't be all that it could be
until you become as great as you can be!***

This is a universal Truth of being human.

A Note on My Writing Style

I think and write like a physical System Science type and that is not the format that most of my readers are expecting to see. In physical System Science it is recognized that there are usually many options to consider; not just two as we are led to assume. To deal with many options, we system types tend to write about the complexity before we focus in on a few options. We are also inclined to go off on tangents! LoL

I use two types of symbols to warn you of my adding new possibilities; one is the semicolon ";" and the other is the long dash ".–.". Sometimes both show up in a single sentence! I also use Capital letters to indicate that I am talking about a Set of related items. The Set of thoughts and emotions called 'Fear' includes the subsets of hate, anger, rage and even fear.

I use single parenthesis to indicate that the enclosed word likely has an unusual meaning so you are warned to take the time to determine what that meaning may be in context. A Capitalized word can also be one that refers to an organization, say a Religion.

Most System Science documents should be scanned the first time through, then read slowly a second time so that you can start to develop a deeper meaning of the idea.

If you do that you will be way ahead of those who just wade through one time only.

The Story To Be Told

Most large organizations are terribly inefficient because of the havoc created by a few bureaucrats who are located at strategic locations along the chain of command. These bureaucrats try to prevent anything getting done. They are afraid of being named if anything goes wrong, so they delay the required tasks ever being started, let alone completed, just so that this sort of blame could never fall on them. They increase the cost of getting things done by not just a few percent, but sometimes by hundreds of percentage points. In the end, they slow progress terribly and can easily make the organization so inefficient that it cannot survive (except for governments, who then destroy the economy of whole countries). All this is done in Fear and without any concern about what they have done to destroy organizations, progress and society at large.

Most organizations do scapegoat those involved in failed ventures, but a sufficiently skilled and immoral person can find ways to avoid being targeted, by ensuring that they have paperworked their part of things to the point where only the truly-interested can see through the paperwork fortress. A blocking bureaucrat can become organizationally powerful, even dominant, especially if they are in league with others along the chain. Their skills at hiding their villainy can be legend.

By dotting 't's and crossing 'i's, and other nonsensical processes, they can reject a whole string of adequate submissions from getting upper management support of getting the approval for needed action. Since there will be no obvious logic in why the rejection occurs, they cannot usually be outwitted, except by those who finally understand what is going on. By then, the talented ones have either given up, gone into survival mode, or moved on. Loss of these competent ones is just one of the real costs of this ludicrous behavior. A common justification for lack of progress will be the complaint of incompetent underlings, although that is highly unlikely to be the truth – truth being seen as a bad thing under such conditions.

Such blocks can usually best be found from the bottom up, but one will normally be dealing with those who are dispirited, or presently apathetic. In reality, just about everyone knows who the offenders are, but they will also know how vicious that they are as well. Good questionnaires and protocols, plus clever investigators with good cover stories, may be needed to both find the culprits and solidify their evidence. Some questions may prove to be critical ones and should be carefully crafted. Ways of dealing with blockage from the offenders will be needed for sure.

Any proper assessment of the real cost to the organization, because of the existence and action of these blocking bureaucrats, will indicate that these costs are huge; not only in time and money but in morale and the timeliness of effective action. The costs of removing these blocks will be truly minute compared to the cost of leaving them in place. Removal, however, should done with due consideration of possible lawsuits, since all blocking bureaucrats will want to avoid the infamy of being named as the reason for poor organizational performance. Finding replacements who will enthusiastically find ways of getting the job done should not be a problem. Good retraining and improved policy and procedures manuals will certainly be required.

These Bureaucrats Are Lethal

Most organizations have one or more reasons for existence. Providing a service (even if it is just a product that provides a service) is an important part of that organization's 'Raison D'Etre.' If the service is delivered late at great expense, or of poor quality, the organization may not thrive. If all of the above faults happen, total collapse may well occur – although many levels of government survive by simply driving their economies into the ground, while doing nothing on time or within budget; or ever fully-meeting service needs.

One reason for all of these failures occurring is that many organizations have one or more bureaucrats who are in critical positions along the chain of command. These persons act as effective blocks to getting anything done efficiently and effectively. They are often highly effective at what they do, are virtually impossible to bypass, and are highly skilled at both hiding their real purposes and preventing their easy removal; or even relocation to less critical positions. They intentionally gravitate to those locations that are critical for getting approval for needed action; then prevent or seriously delay any progress. They

11

may not hold senior positions but they do wield great power.

An Expensive Kind Of Bureaucrat

When such blocking bureaucrats are in place, the length of time it takes to accomplish any mandated task can be increased several-fold. The cost of that delay is often magnified by a required increase in the number of staff needed to get the job done later. Such bureaucrats also tend to destroy the morale of those both above and below them; but they usually have developed techniques for being 'Teflon-coated' when blame for a delay or cost over-run is assigned. One of their skills in in finding ways to make it look as though subordinates were to blame, or superiors, or likely both. It is this skill (when used over time) that is so demoralizing to the whole organization.

When we think of cost or time over-runs, we usually try to find reasons for effects in the few percent to several tens of percent range. Such a blocking bureaucrat can increase delivery time and overall cost by many times (or in the several-hundred-percent increase category). If you are looking for a few percent you may not see a few hundred percent. Such an effect is simply not conceivable to most of us; so is therefore not even considered. Someone famous once said "Those who have eyes, let them see!" and it is difficult to step back far enough for anyone to 'see' effects that are so huge. System Scientists, however, do this all of the time. The Author was a physical System Scientist before he retired. His primary skills are in seeing the big picture and helping others ask better questions.

Why They Behave Like That

One of the driving characteristics of a blocking-bureaucrat is a fear of ever doing wrong; or being seen to do wrong. 'No action allowed' might prevent them being blamed for things that often go wrong in any organizations run by humans. Even when the CEO has mandated that the whole organization gets a certain task done within a certain timeframe, within budget and with an adequate quality, such blocking bureaucrats see that as a license to subvert important procedures that effectively prevent them from being seen to have made a mistake – if one is ever allowed to happen. A Fear of making a mistake, or worse still to be seen to have been actively involved in the making of such a mistake, is a totally unacceptable situation to any blocking-bureaucrat. Preventing all progress is seen as justifiable, if that is the way to prevent being assigned some responsibility in any possible mistake happening (even if the probability is very low – to almost zero).

Most humans (96%) are still living in the thinking but fearful mode. Many others do not even believe that there is anything like a real Truth in this universe (85%). Under these circumstances there is no personal connection to either Truth nor to the essential value of other persons or things. If you do **not** believe that there is any real Truth, the smartest person is likely to be the best liar. Protecting one's own butt is more important than protecting the organization for which one works. Taking risks to protect the greater good is a fool's errand; not all of us realize that we humans and our organizations often act like fools.

One who is functioning in a blocking-bureaucrat position in an organization does not (and may never) believe that they are being anything but very clever indeed. To realize this likely truth is vital to clearing them out of troubled organizations.

Their Ongoing Damage To The Organization

This particular type of problem employee does very significant damage because they end up severely stressing the other employees who are there with an intention to get the job done, as requested by Senior Management. Many of us are both consciously and subconsciously driven to serve and feel helpless when we do our best and yet that that work is rejected – often for no good reason as we see it. If Senor Management has not seen and corrected the problem created by the blocker, it may be that the employee whose work is rejected starts to wonder if all of management above that level is not of the same ilk. If the good ones do not leave at this point, and many don't leave physically but do so emotionally and intellectually, then they will settle for doing a less-than-effective job. This is one hell of a way to run a railroad! LoL.

Anyone whose work causes even a temporary loss of commitment to the organization is doing great damage to it. Those who cause longer-term decreases in commitment, and yet stay in their powerful positions, do untold damage. It has always been a mystery to the author why such lower-management employees are left in place, because surely someone is noticing that the organization is not doing as well as it should be doing. Maybe that is not in anyone's mandate.

Then again, although the author was given a great deal of management training, he was never impressed with what he was taught (or by those who taught him). He got good grades (usually ranked as 'excellent'), but could not force himself to adopt the immoral methods taught to him. That training often focused on making ourselves look good to our superiors, and on feeding their weaknesses and egos – getting the requested job done well was never even mentioned. Again and again I was told that senior management did not want to be told the Truth, but only that things were going as well as could be expected.

When he looked around himself, he saw a great deal of unhappiness in other employees who had also hired on to be good contributors, not just for the money. They too lost at least some of their drive over time, when the blocker was left in position, even though the group was not doing as well as we knew that we could do. This effect resulted in quite a few 'sick' days after a strong push to get a submission to management was returned with almost mindless comments; as well as requests for changes that were often just a minor revision in style. It is difficult to be impressed with Senior Management who needs to be fed only a type of pap, delivered in only one possible way. The cost of this sort of deterioration of respect for upper-middle and Senior Management is likely hard to measure – but it should be estimated ruthlessly anyway.

How They Have Arisen In Organizations

Although many who work for governments joined to be of service to society, most of government is not now run that way (if it ever was). All bureaucracies ultimately ignore the founding reasons for their coming into being in the first place, and are changed into organizations that are there primarily to serve the needs of the bureaucrats. Without regular house cleaning, sometimes brutal ones if a thorough review of operations is not done regularly, more and more activities have no useful purpose in delivering the service (or product, which then supplies the service) for which that organization really exists. Their purpose becomes simply to give everyone something to do and to further the power needs of some middle management personnel. It would seem that this situation is either not fully understood by most Senior Management, or is implicitly (or even explicitly), supported. In any case, nothing seems to get done to correct such problems.

The usual salary structure, which depends upon salary level being a function of the number of employees being supervised (and not the properly-defined output that is to be achieved) is a major contributor to over-bloating. That could surely be the subject of another publication!

Avoiding Getting Blamed For Problems

If we live in the states of Fear, and most of us do, we do not like being involved in things that are going wrong; and especially do not like being blamed even as a part of a group. One way to avoid that unpleasant and often threatening situation is to make sure that others are set up to take the fall. If we can blame underlings for not doing their part, or supervisors for either not being clear enough about expectations or providing enough resources, we might appear to be off the hook. Those bureaucrats who block progress on any task, until it is obvious that the project is finally going to have to go ahead anyway, usually have all the documentation in place in the case that things do go wrong.

If you successfully prevent that task from even getting going it obviously cannot go wrong.

Of course if the task was vital to a bigger project, the whole project is incomplete but that impact is never of any concern to those who simply want to avoid blame. Others may be concerned about this kind of failure to perform, but that is either above or well below the pay grade of a blocking-bureaucrat. Being successful in preventing something going forward is success in avoiding blame for a possible failure. In many experiences with such persons, they had no functional understand of probability and saw even a minor possibility of a problem arising as unacceptable. They were sure that this 'possibility' would inevitably cause devastation, and then a great deal of blaming would be a certain result. If it were in any way possible to such as these, that meant that it would definitely go wrong. Discussions about the probability being very low were simply not heard, since those arguing for low probabilities were obviously not very worldly-wise and just did not understand how things really happen.

When you live in the states of Fear, everything that can go wrong will go wrong; any opinion to the contrary is nonsensical! To a blocking-bureaucrat, only very foolish optimists believe differently!

Becoming Dominant But Invisible

It is important to realize that anyone who succeeds in becoming an effective blocking-bureaucrat is smart in some important aspects of surviving in a bureaucracy. To underestimate their cunning is to make a very great mistake! They are survivors or they would not continue to be a problem. Two of the skills that they need to become effective in this role are to become a dominant part of the hierarchy of the approval process, yet to be virtually invisible to those not yet skilled at finding them. Since their impact on the organization is so powerfully negative, it is important that they not be too visible.

For good reasons, the requests for approval to act, submitted from the lower layers where the real action will occur, has to be couched in a format and 'language set' that senior officers are both used to and can understand. Some of middle management become efficient in seeing what will 'fly' and what will not.

They could just correct what is submitted to them, check to make sure that they have not changed the intent or context in any way, and then pass it on up. That, however, would make them extremely vulnerable if anything ever went wrong in that project. There is a safer way. Send it back, with very few clues as to what is wrong, insult the intelligence and skills of those who just want to get on with the task to be done, and then wait for a resubmission. Since the comments were doubly-negative, it will be a while before the workers will come up with a new version. That will then be criticized, often with conflicting comments about the failings of this version in comparison with the last one; the process will then be repeated. Nothing gets approved and most involved get hurt and dispirited; but there is no action going on so the blocking-bureaucrat is still safe.

Finally, senior levels will get impatient and ask why nothing has come up for approval. It is at this point that a version is sent up, usually with excuses about the incompetence of the originating underlings, and the project goes ahead even though it is likely already well behind schedule. It is at this point that the blocking bureaucrat organizes everything for the possible witch hunt that might come later; if something goes wrong in the implementation phase. If a program is set up as a series of projects, this can go on for a very long time – but the middle managers will not be seen to be the real reason for the length of time and resources consumed.

The Implications Of Several Layers

When there are two such persons in any chain of command, things can go terribly wrong and the company or organization can be destroyed. In physical systems, this is often modeled as 'n' to the power 'n,' and just two of such personnel ends up being four times as bad as one. If a third is added, as happens in some government agencies, the effect is 27 times as bad. Without regular shake-ups this can really happen. It is possible that The Vatican of the

Roman Catholic Church suffers from this level of such a malady.

The only hope here is that the ones sent in to solve the problem are ruthless in their weeding out of the offenders. Even if you miss one of the three the problem becomes dramatically less. (For those who wondered, if there are four of them in line, the problem would be 256 times as bad as just one. The worse the problem the more important it becomes to weed out as many as you can find). The locating and weeding out process does not increase the need for resources, according to this law, but just goes up linearly. Cheer up, for there is always hope. Also, if this is done on a regular basis it may be possible to get them all; therefore getting the number remaining down to zero!

How They Are Making Success Difficult

As an expansion on what you may well have already guessed, the blocking process is rather simple, although it may not be visible until you look for it. We have to make assumptions when we try to get anything done and one of the assumptions is that those who are not 'on side' will be noticed and dealt with as a normal process of management. That is only occasionally true, however, and bad assumptions are usually the reason for most failures to perform. To repeat; it is the assumptions made, and not the effort to get the job done that are at fault!

There are three ways that blocking is made successful: causing things to go in circles (recycling) is one; successfully blaming underlings is the second; and, redefining the value systems naively assumed by senior management to be at work through the organization is the third – this third way can be deadly!

Recycling The Processes Of Approval

There are advantages to wheels that endlessly go round and round, but in the approval process for programs, projects or tasks that senior management wants done, this should not become one of those processes of interminable recycling steps – with no end in sight. The very-accomplished blocking-bureaucrat can set such an approvals or information process into something that looks just like a forever-ongoing circle of events. It is only when senior management finally sends down angry-sounding requests for progress that it will be removed from the circular process and a response will be sent along. A way of avoiding blame would have been long ago developed and now put into action!

Successfully Blaming Underlings

One of the skills, and an extremely destructive one to employee morale, is that the blocking bureaucrat will have developed ways of directing blame to incompetent subordinates; from whom they have valiantly struggled to get an adequate response. Unless Senior Management is more sensitive than most, the story will be presented in a very convincing fashion; with enough details included to make further investigation an obviously-unnecessary task. The reality that it is mostly a fabrication will be carefully kept from sight. The right skills can make this story so well presented that the real perpetrator will be hard to find from above.

From below, the whole process will be much more obvious. Only a few subordinates keep sufficiently-detailed records however, so that the one who is being blamed by the blocking-bureaucrat may not withstand attack from the one truly responsible for the delay. This issue is addressable however, but only by those who understand the process and are truly interested in finding a way to make the organization more effective and efficient.

A Redefinition Of Value

One of the problems with blocking bureaucrats is that they become very good at changing the values that senior management believe to be both well-known in their original form, and consistently-used throughout the chain of command. The new value system is all about developing a paperwork process that protects the blocking bureaucrat. It also values the uncertain and never-fully-communicated standards for a well-crafted submission or report. As long as the rules for what is needed are never precisely presented in written format, the rules can be changed both at will (and as necessary) to prevent any requested documentation from getting past the blocker.

Getting the job done to senior management's cost and timeline requirements is not any part of the modified process. Those who try to meet senior managements requested targets are prevented from doing so. They are also made to feel helpless in dealing with the roadblocks that are consistently presented; no matter how hard they try to meet the requirements originated by Senior Management.

When successfully meeting undefined and purposefully-variable style, content and value requirements becomes impossible (because this is the unstated purpose of a blocking bureaucrat) those trying to get the job done will have their morale and self-confidence destroyed. This may occur to most, or all of those who are subordinate to the bureaucrat in question. Those who refuse to knuckle under are often singled out for discredit, by lies and ridicule throughout the middle management organization. This can be effective and terribly-demoralizing. Few survive it. Many move out, or finally capitulate. The author left! He never should have done so, as it turns out, but it seemed necessary for his emotional and mental survival at the time!

How To Find Them

Not all blocking bureaucrats are obvious to those who are not one of their subordinates, but it is through those whose work is delayed that you can find them. They may be hard to see from above, but from both a side view and the view from below, they can be found quickly.

One of the indispensable tools for finding blockage is the organization chart. It provides a wonderful ability to 'see' the flow of paperwork, if you draw it out and ask enough questions to confirm that you have the paperwork flow process correctly displayed. If you ask innocuous questions about how things work, using no wording that could be interpreted as judgemental, it is not too difficult to develop a 'picture' of the flow of the approval processes, and then to confirm that you have it correctly charted. One of the tools that any investigator must have is an assurance that the present and past organization charts are complete, and also that the names of those filling the positions are correct; not only now but in past versions. For someone to become a blocking bureaucrat, they have to be high enough in the chain of command, but also relatively long-term in a position, or in one just above or below it. The paperwork flow must go through them if they are to block progress.

One caution in this charting process is that there are both the names for all 'positions' and the names of the 'persons of those who fill the positions.' Position names often change, but a bit of work can show whether or not the functions have changed in any way that is critical to the flow of approval to proceed with a task, project or program of projects. Part of the camouflage process may be a change of position name, while the control function remains the same. Ultimately it is the control functions that matter.

A list of questions to be asked, to ensure that the investigator really does understand the nature and location of the functions, should be developed and updated frequently. Before they are actually used, the questions have to be fine-tuned and polished but they should be identified early on in any investigation.

Interviewing Subordinates

There will be an array of attitudes present in any organization that is plagued by blocking bureaucrats. Such persons cause very serious emotional, mental and spiritual problems for those who must deal with them, and the process does leave many injuries. These are dealt with using a variety of coping mechanisms. Some of the ones who are hurt get angry, or even depressed; some simply fail to care anymore; some find other reasons for keeping on keeping on, and some leave (or are planning to leave later). Subordinates who show any of these coping mechanisms can be helpful; if approached in the right way.

Some have become turtles and show no visible signs of having to survive in an organization where survival is way more difficult than most think that it should be. You may get nothing from the turtles, unless you can get them to tell anecdotes about what has happened to others. Here they can become quite helpful indeed!

One thing that will always be a problem is that most of the subordinates have been taught to fear retaliation from the blocking-bureaucrat, as well as the friends of such bureaucrats who are higher up. Fearful people have to be provided with safe passage, not just some appearances of safe passage. They will demand real, reliable assurances. That may not be possible until after the housecleaning has been finished for a while, with the possibility that the damage is permanent for some of the most injured and fearful. Still, one can try and see what works.

One of realities of this universe is that our expectations may not come close to what we experience. Some results will be better than we expected and some

Bureaucrats Who Block Progress

lesser, but being loving while chasing down responses is never the wrong thing to do.

The Critical Questions

There are a myriad of questions that could be asked while trying to locate the blocking-bureaucrat, but they generally conform to the following types:

1. **Do you**, or someone you know, have to apply for approval to act on a task, project, or program of projects?

2. **Do you** fully understand the way that the request is channeled up through management, to have that approval processed?

3. **Are there** some persons or management positions that regularly request changes to the submission, before it is passed on up the chain?

4. **How long** does it take for that request for changes to get back to you (a range of times would be helpful)?

5. **Does the request** come back with a list of helpful comments as to how the submission could be improved?

6. **Is the request** couched in positive, negative or both types of comments?

7. **What is the range** in the number of such requests for changes that must be made on any given submission?

8. **How long** does it take you to do the requested revisions, both in calendar time and man-hours of effort?

9. **Do you feel** fully engaged in other required tasks while you are waiting for approval?

10.**If there** is a drop in your effectiveness, can you estimate what that drop in effectiveness would be, in both man-hours ineffectively used and the length of time over which that change occurs?

11.**Do you believe** that your understanding of the situation is similar to what others hold?

12.**Do you believe** that Senior Management fully understands the process as it is actually occurring?

13.**Do you believe** that there are similar persons doing the same things higher up the chain of command?

14.**Do you know** of any of your associates who have shut down or left, partly as a result of frustration over this process?

15.**Was their loss** in this process a significant blow to the organization?

It is likely that the tone of these questions should be significantly improved and polished by professionals, so as to be less leading if that is possible. Over time, all such questions should be reviewed, even split tested to improve accuracy. It is possible however, that the proposed bureaucratic-blocker problem is big enough that it should be solved right away, rather than being made into a whole new round of delaying tactics.

Avoiding Snow Jobs

One of the things that is going to happen, to anyone who attempts to correct a blocking-bureaucrat problem, is that there will be many who have already rehearsed what to do to prevent corrective action from happening; or they have been taught how to respond through fear-generating mechanisms. Just being aware that this is the way that it is might be enough to prevent the investigator from being the victim of snow jobs that prevent the acquisition of good data and information. Many middle managers have been through corporate communication training that teaches them several communication techniques, namely: a) never answer the question being asked, but rather provide an answer to the question that you prefer would have been asked; b) never tell the truth, unless you absolutely have to, since lies can always be changed as needed, but the Truth will stand on its own merit; c) attack the questioner to get them to back off; and, d) start off on a new tack if at all possible. While this list is anything but exhaustive, it does provide some cautions that should be considered when dealing with middle management personnel.

It is never a good idea to get snowed but not know it! It may happen no matter what you do but your report can indicate where that happened, if it did occur and by whom. Some Senior Management personnel will have to deal with this snow job, or the impact of such behavior. Hopefully they will understand the impacts of being snowed by those who have done so; or who have been cowed by it.

It is likely that being specific in this area might have to be done in an undocumented fashion, one-on-one with those who commissioned the investigation. It may be wise to have this privately discussed at the start of the project. See also the last subsection of the next chapter.

How To Deal With Them

Any blocking-bureaucrat worth their salt is going to have their defenses rehearsed and in place, long before any investigation as to their existence and impact takes place. Removing, or shunting such power-mad persons into positions where they can no longer cause as much damage, should always be done with the understanding that defensive situations have already been put into place; perhaps a very long time ago. All such people have been driven by fear-like emotions (often not conscious ones, though) and any approach to unseat them will unleash fear-driven responses against any and all attempted actions of removal or relocation.

It makes good sense to start any investigation with a clear understanding that any corrective actions will result in retaliation, or other forms of prevention of change. Although this should be done beforehand it is highly-likely that it should be done 'in camera' as it were.

Even if the whole process of investigation and resolution is done quickly, and in an unobtrusive manner, there will be a time when defensive reactions will be started; by not only those who are ultimately targeted but also by their compatriots, both friendly to them or deeply afraid of the blocking-bureaucrat. In some ways, this can be seen as a war, but more of a guerrilla version than an out-in-the-open one. Any campaign that does not recognize this reality, or fully-address this possibility, will fail; perhaps catastrophically!

Estimating Their Real Cost Impact

If you asked most senior management if there were any such personnel in their organizations, you might not get a clear response, one way or another. For those who suspected that there were some, when you asked about their impact, it is likely that they would say that they might increase costs, and time taken, by a few percent. They might also say that if they had the time it might be worthwhile dealing with them. In some organizations the impact is likely not in the percentage category, but in the 'times 2+ area (hundreds of percent).' In many very large organizations, especially governments, it may be that their impact is well above 2 times as much time taken and costs incurred, for the approvals process stream in which they work. In some cases they affect costs and time taken in all parts of the organization. If that is so, then it is going to be very important that they be identified and their negative effects be removed as soon and completely as possible.

The only reliable final costing will occur when such blocking bureaucrats are dealt with in such a way that even their lingering damage has been healed. That does not mean however, that a good-enough estimate cannot be develop in short order.

Much of the information gathered during any investigation will make it possible to develop fairly-reliable numbers as to the delays caused by the presence of such blocking processes. Even a crude estimate of how long it should take to get the approval process expedited will likely be a much smaller number, compared to what time and manpower impacts exist at the moment. My personal experience, plus those discussed in other departments of federal governments, would place delays in the orders of several months, with those employees whose initial submissions were rejected often becoming virtually ineffective for weeks on end. In some cases it takes half a year or so.

The 'right' questions, when asked earlier, could coax out answers to how long it took for each rewrite and how many rewrites were eventually required. With this information, and an updated understanding of just how the processes flowed in the organization, useful estimates of impact should be quickly obtainable.

It should be noted that the priority for all such estimates is as follows:

1) is it a positive or negative number?;
2) where is the decimal place in both the times and the costs?;
3) what is the first significant number?; and,
4) is there really any need to go further?

If an answer is that the existing costs in time and effort are 200+% of what they could be if the system were both efficient and effective, then there may be no need to get more accuracy in this process. If the results are 3%, then no action may be needed, so finding out that a better estimate of 3.3% is just wasted time and effort, therefore wasted costs.

It is highly likely that once such an investigation has been done well and on time, it can be done more accurately, quickly and reliably when repeated, either in other organizations, or in search for other blocking bureaucrats in the same organization. It is only when the best estimates show a direct cost that is in the few percentage range that no further effort is required.

It is worth repeating that the indirect costs may only be available after a major change has been implemented and time has allowed some healing in the organization;

before really reliable numbers are available. If the indirect costs are as large as the author suspects that they are, they will be both important and rough estimates of impact may be largely transferable to other situations. People within an organization may be hurt and heal in different ways. Over time it might be possible to make some rather reliable predictions as to what is going on in many organizations of similar structure.

Of note is the possibility that those companies who work **for** government agencies may have similar cost-increasing processes at work within their organizations. Once some sort of confidence is developed at the funding-supply level, it may be beneficial to require a similar investigation within contractor firms, etc.

Determining The Cost Of Replacing Them

If done correctly and with adequate resolve, it should be possible to determine the replacement costs of filling a vacated position with someone who is not going to just set up a new version of the old problem. Any delay in carrying out the replacement however, could result in a considerable increase in ancillary damage to others affected, so the costs of delay might also be a required item in determining replacement costs.

All in all however, determination of replacement costs should be pretty straight forward, especially if all of the investigation information is used in selecting a proactive replacement. At this stage it is highly unlikely that the whole organization does not know what is going on, so those affected will be looking for a very different type of person to step into the position and make their lives easier. It is possible, of course, that just replacing the problem bureaucrat with a person with a very different style will have quite a good rebound effect. That may be worth recording, for the future.

Avoiding Removal And Replacement Problems

Given a situation where those who are removed for even the best of reasons are already thinking that they are the offended ones (and given that some lawyers are willing to take on very shaky cases for the publicity value), it may be that other parts of the organization could and should be working on an update to any existing removal processes. To be forearmed might be a very good thing in this situation. The caution, of course, is all such efforts have to be done in relative secrecy. If handled externally, development of options and recommendations may be one way to keep things from feeding the grapevine. There need be no requirement to be specific about the reasons for removal, but only that it cover a range of possible employee responses.

Preparedness may be quite important here as the one removed may be a very effective infighter or they would not have done so much damage!

The Story Retold

Those who live in a 'thinking but fearful' mode are everywhere and some have done terrible things to the efficiency and effectiveness of most large and very-large organizations. When located in critical locations within the middle management positions of larger organizations, they try very hard to avoid being blamed if and when things go wrong; in tasks, projects and programs of projects. They do this by preventing anything getting done; at least as long as they can do so. I call these persons 'blocking-bureaucrats' and they can dramatically increase the time and money costs (by many times) of senior-management instructions to get things done. These particular bureaucrats have no interest in what Senior Management wants to get done; they are only interested in being kept safe from having to accept any blame when things go wrong.

It is my belief that the size of the calendar time and man-hour costs of their activities is enormous, in some cases, but not necessarily identified and understood. In large government, it may much more than double (even triple or more) the time to completion of some jobs and even triple (or more) the man-hour costs (through personal

41

observation of all of this presently going on). The same is likely happening in large industries. When large government contract with large industrial companies, the combination may be worse than a simple additive effect. Solving this proposed problem would then produce enormous savings and allow much more to be done, much more quickly, with the same dollar total! The time has surely come for efficiencies to be put into place – soon!

Blocking bureaucrats often cause recycling of requests for approval to get things done by using purposefully obtuse instructions for rewrites, when the original document was 'good enough' as submitted (or could easily have been 'polished' by that bureaucrat and sent along the chain of command). That is not done however, as it would leave them vulnerable for some blame if anything ever went wrong. If you believe that everything always goes wrong, this is an untenable situation for you. Blocking and setting up the ability to blame subordinates is what is being done. The trouble is that just about everyone else becomes dispirited and inefficient. Usually the costs in lost time and wasted man-hours is not a few percent, but maybe hundreds of percent for that part of the chain of approval.

If several such bureaucrats exist in one chain the effects can be modeled and the costs become extreme.

Such bureaucrats are most easily located from the bottom up. With the development and field trial of proper procedures, locating and documenting these blocking bureaucrats should be relatively easy; what might not be easy is preventing their defensive actions, which could seriously decrease the efficiency of subordinates and damage to morale may already be high.

Removal of these persons, as well as repair of the organization is possible; but only if the correct procedures are developed and then used ruthlessly. If the problems are solved, much more could be done in time and within similar or lower budgets; but only if action is both swift and decisive.

In government contracting, it may be very helpful to insist that a similar activity be set in place within the contractor's organization. Results could be outstanding!

What Comes Next?

The author believes that we as humans in damaged societies cannot afford to continue to leave blockages to efficient and effective progress in place. Others may beg to differ, while others will go into defensive attack mode. In those cases, it will be useful to note and catalogue those who are vicious in reaction to any calls for change! We might consider 'Bolding' the names of those who are really nasty! When corrective action is needed, start out Boldly!

Our egos really dislike change since they do not yet have working corrective actions in place for any new ways. Egos do not care if a change is going to make something better or worse (and may not even use those considerations in their response processes). To our individual egos (and to those parts of society that act in ego-like ways) all change 'could be' dangerous. There is no significant need for a high **probability** of a problem, only the **possibility** of one (and a minute possibility will always exist). The problem here is that we humans succeed by getting the probabilities right, sometimes even by shading the choice to act by intentionally going into situations that really could blow up in our faces. Doing nothing will almost certainly have a bad outcome in such cases. Hey, we are still here, so such decisions are sometimes valid. Good Leaders make these choices all of the time!

Learning Who the Blockers Are

Blocking Bureaucrats do significant damage to organizations but they can do crippling damage to subordinates; or anyone who is lower in the chain of command used for approval for tasks, projects or programs of projects. When your request to be given 'approval to act' is nearly always rejected, this will be a blow to our opinion of our self-worth and expertise. Too many such blows will do significant emotional and mental damage and some of it may be permanent. For this reason those who block approval are well known by those who have trouble getting requests for action approved. Blocking bureaucrats are always known by those whom they frustrate! This is the place to start!

It is important to note, however, that those who have been most affected may have reacted by: leaving the organization; arranging for a lateral transfer; becoming fearful of all interactions when this is the subject; or just becoming reluctant to discuss the problem. Only a few will still be willing to stand up and tell it like it is.

Any successful blocking bureaucrat will already have processes in place to read the pulse of any activity that could affect them, or they would likely already have been moved or otherwise eliminated. Although it may be impossible to completely prevent defensive actions being taken as soon as an activity is set up to discover who they are, ways of teasing out those activities should be a part of any protocol used by the organization and the investigators.

To properly identify who is blocking progress, the team will have to develop investigative protocols that deal with the above problems in a sensitive way while, at the same time, getting enough high-quality information as to all who are involved in the process of delaying progress. After the first few uses of these protocols, they may become quite well developed.

Senior Management will have to develop methods of keeping the real purpose for new activities sufficiently vague and wide-ranging, so that the intended targets do not have too much warning as to what is really going on. Certainly they should be aware of (and properly track) sources, if there are disciplinary action requests from those where blocking could occur. Frightening, then following through on punishing those who do provide good information to investigators, is a possible (even probable) defensive activity of those are being targeted!

It is highly likely that development of all protocols, and all report writing, should be done off-site!

Confirming That All Are Identified

In some bigger organizations, it is likely that there is more than one blocking-bureaucrat in the management chain that allows action to be taken at the working levels. If it is really true, this can be modeled as an 'n' to the power of 'n' process, where finding even one makes a great difference but finding more would turn a very-badly-struggling organization into an efficient and effective one. If Senior Management is going to commission an investigation and remediation task, the scope should likely include rapid identification of all 'suspects' from the get-go.

Once the investigative team has managed to get to the level of the lowest blockage they will almost certainly be able to 'guess' (Intuition is actually very real and very powerful indeed) just who is blocking further up the chain of command and control. Anyone who performs as an investigator is going to be 'hooked' at this stage, and may have trouble keeping their activities sufficiently-well masked so that they are not 'seen' by all concerned. At this stage however, the likelihood of defensive action helping to pinpoint those involved is very good indeed. Once the cat is out of the bag, even well-scripted defenses may be done a little too emotionally to stay within logic-based patterns that were intended to hide those who are blocking progress. We humans sometimes let emotion destroy the most logic-based defensive plans and activities.

The only serious problem that could occur at this stage would be a lack of resolve to see the process through by Senior Management. In the end that will not work and the investigation team should not concern themselves with this possibility, although they should just go ahead and get done what can be done. Hopefully the investigators were chosen in light of the fact that some pretty nasty things would be said about them, as well as the horse that they ride in upon (their firm). That is historically predictable, but has not stopped many valiant warriors!

Removing The Offenders

Once the real cost of having blocking-bureaucrats has been determined and their identity exposed, there are several options open to Senior Management: a) offer them an early-retirement package (with stipulations on what they can, and cannot, say to others); b) insist that they retire, or be fired; c) move them laterally, all the while putting surveillance processes in place to minimize their future damage; and, d) promote them to a position with no power over anyone, but also keeping their verbal interactions with others well-managed.

All of these options have advantages and disadvantages.

Especially if more than one such bureaucrat is discovered, a re-organization that covers what is really intended could be drafted by either senior management, or, better-yet, offered to Senior Management by the investigative team. The covering contract to the investigating company could well require that a well-defined 'subordinate healing process' be a part of the recommendations.

Rebuilding With Those Who Get Things Done

Humans have always been driven by both selfish and altruistic motives. Many who enter large companies desire both money and the ability to make a difference. At the moment, the human species is exponentially evolving towards a more loving and altruistic mode of being – this is true even if not well presented by a press that is being well-paid to prevent this process from being discovered and publicized.

Because of this evolution, there are many who would love to do a job that was both well-paid and offered a chance to help the organizations that they work within to become both efficient and effective in delivering what Senior Management asks to be done. When they joined the organization, it may have been with a wildly optimistic view of what they could do; and even what Senior Management really wanted done.

What is special here is that any Senior Management team that hires investigators to make the present organization more efficient and effective is also likely to be interested in developing a long-term plan that helps the organization survive and thrive during changing times.

We live in interesting times, which the Chinese considered a curse, but leaders can achieve great things; if they see rapidly-changing situations as perfect for moving an existing organization into a much-more-relevant and important role in the future.

Blocking-bureaucrats were never concerned about the organization and its mandate. Once they are no longer active it may well be that great changes can be made. Making good money while efficiently and effectively delivering a useful service is going to be a good thing for all involved. With the right mindset, it can certainly be seen as a morally-correct viewpoint as well!

**It was the love of money, not money itself,
that was called evil!
Most of us have been misinformed about this!**

The Author

You should always know something about anyone who proposes to teach or show you something of value. Something of me follows.

I was trained as a scientist, but in an Engineering faculty – this sort of training is best suited for those who might like to help transfer new Science into new Engineering practice, or help move new answers into more common practice. It is short on specifics and long on basics, including the need to question everything, even (or especially) the questions and founding assumptions. My basic Bachelor of Applied Science degree (Aeronautical Option) was used to its fullest in eight different fields, but was of most use in aircraft and spacecraft component design. In most cases I worked at the physical System Science level, although occasionally doing detail design, development, testing and product approval activities.

In the spacecraft area, I performed not only a thorough review of the systems design of the Canadarm on the US Space Shuttle, but co-authored the detail design of the six joints of that complex electromechanical mechanism. For that project I worked with Canada's best gearing system designer. I learned a lot, but also brought a fresh perspective to some of the processes involved.

When the test results of the engineering model of one of the similar joints did not come close to fitting the textbook equations for this sort of drive system, I was asked to develop a new set of equations from basic Science and Mathematics (and our evolving understanding of friction processes). The resulting equation set both better fit the data and allowed the development of a much simpler control system design. My skeptical attitude helped a lot here especially my willingness to question founding assumptions.

When working in the field of housing and health, I also learned a great deal about how our ongoing limitations, in our social and societal processes, resist our doing what was 'right' and rather lead us towards choosing what was selfish and anti-life. Here the System Science questions were more widely based and the errors of our ways were more devastating for mankind, and for the beautiful blue planet that gives us the opportunity of a great life.

While trying to get warring committee members to better understand the possible interpretations of the accepted indoor air quality equations, I developed a new way of processing that complex equation, in the end supporting the positions taken by several industry and scientific communities – there were many ways of looking at both the processes involved, and how those processes interacted and ranked in importance. When this was presented, however, it was ridiculed (although supported by several leading Canadian mathematicians) as being mathematically and physically incorrect and incompetent. It soon became obvious that several members did not want any of the others involved to have a valid position. What they wanted was to be 'Right' and everyone else had to be wrong. Others being wrong was the most important point for both them and their industry associations

Over time I generalized that position as showing up in many ways, in many groups. In some cases even a good physical System Scientist could not help forge a consensus, because none was desired, or would ever be allowed!

In another case, however, a large committee of those with very different positions to present, on behalf of their industry groups, finally agreed that a consensus had been reached and that the public and the industry groups involved should be formally informed of that situation. Shortly after the meeting at which that consensus was reached, the committee was dissolved at the request of the Minister responsible for that agency, at the request of one of the industry associations. As a result, we still have inadequate standards and less than healthy housing when our houses could be so much better at a very reasonable cost; a net decrease in total housing-related, 'health plus housing' set of costs could have been possible with better standards.

What The Author Believes

Having had five heart attacks and two out-of-body experiences, I have taken my previous 'attitude problem' and 'fired' it into a pretty-solid attitude indeed! The following points are relative to this document:

1. **There is Truth** in this universe and the concept of there being only relative (tribal) truths is *false*;

2. **The universe** was created within a Divine Creator and, being in the universe we are always intimately connected to / with that Creator;

3. **We are actually** spiritual beings, made in the image of God, and our human journey gives us many chances to grow in our ability to become loving;

4. **Those fearful ones** who have money, things and power do not want us to understand that our Destiny is to become Loving, not 'thinking but fearful;'

5. **Many of those others** with money and power are now living lives driven by Love; they support all of us becoming much more loving;

6. **Anyone** who lives in the many states of Fear can justify doing fearful things, as being the 'sensible' things to do;

7. **In the end,** we should remember that: "What goes around, comes around!" In the Far East they call that Karma, and it is very real;

8. **Choosing** to do immoral things has terrible consequences and humans can learn proper morality (we are born with an inner knowing); and,

9. **The 'days'** of those who choose to do the 'politically-correct' things are rapidly coming to an end. They are everywhere, however, and will cling to their ways with great tenacity.

Although I normally write on the coming together of Science and 'spirituality component of Philosophy,' the above are becoming very relevant to proper efficiency in large organizations, no matter what your beliefs about spirit. If there really are universal Truths, they will have their day. I believe that this is coming soon. Others do not agree with my viewpoints.

Time, of course, will tell!

References and Further Reading

This book is offered as an opinion piece, with no proof provided. If it schmecks, it does. If it doesn't it will be ignored. Let the tiles fall where they may!

Morally-correct action will likely be the norm in the future. Successful organizations will be the first to change not the last ones.

When we survive in the states of Fear we are concerned with consequences and we do what is convenient!

When we try to live in the states of Love (the future of humankind), we are concerned about Responsibilities and we do what is necessary. That is a totally different game indeed!

The Author's Sites And Books

You may wish to read some of the other books by this author, writing on the coming together of Science and spirituality, as Jesuis Laplume. All can be found on www.amazon.com (search for Books and Jesuis Laplume) or copy and paste

The Author's Web Site
www.jesuislaplume.com
and he can be reached at:
jesuislaplume@gmail.com

The Author's Page On Amazon
www.amazon.com/Jesuis-Laplume/e/B00DCFMZD0
(Note that the 0s are zeros)
(or search for Jesuis Laplume on any Amazon site)

The Author's Books (By Order Published)
"On Life And Love And Why We Are Here
    An Introduction To the New Spirituality
    For Beginners"
"The Affirmation Prayer
    Affirming Who You Really Are!"

Bureaucrats Who Block Progress

Bureaucrats Who Block Progress

"Unconditional Love:

    A Primer"

"Changing The Universe:

    By Changing Yourself"

"You Are A Powerful, Eternal, Spiritual Being:

    You Are One With The One"

"Hate The Sin:

    But Not The Sinner"

Your Notes

www.ingramcontent.com/pod-product-compliance
Lightning Source LLC
Chambersburg PA
CBHW070359190526
45169CB00003B/1045